Mind

Views

Bart Hopkins Jr.

Published by Bart Hopkins Jr.

Galveston, Texas

ISBN-10: 978-1518718250

ISBN-13: 1518718256

First Printing October 2015

To all those interested in the mind, language, and symbols, and for the good readers and seekers everywhere.

Table of Contents

I do not know what I may appear to the world, but to myself I seem to have been only like a boy playing on the sea-shore, and diverting myself in now and then finding a smoother pebble or a prettier shell than ordinary, whilst the great ocean of truth lay all undiscovered before me.

Sir Isaac Newton

Writing fiction is like gliding on air currents. Writing scientific material like this is more similar to guiding a heavily laden vessel through a narrow strait, in rough and perilous seas, with always an iceberg looming off the bow.

Me

Purpose

Since childhood I have been fascinated with the thinking process. How we know what we know. What the brain and the mind are. What the relationship between language and thought is. The basic building blocks of thought and how we put them together. What language is and how it began. What constitutes intelligence.

The following pages are the most satisfactory explanations of these phenomena of which I have knowledge. Much of what follows is a synthesis and expansion of those thinkers noted in the text and listed in the bibliography. This text is not exhaustive, by any means, but only the bare outlines of an introduction to these subjects. Though I hope scientists can enjoy it also, the material is written on a level that should appeal to the interested and curious layman who already possesses some background knowledge of the brain, symbols, concepts, language, and the processes of the mind.

An ulterior motive for writing these pages was to organize what I have learned from others and my own thoughts into some kind of coherent whole. There is an anecdote about Richard Feynman, in which an interlocutor questions him about his thinking. Does he have the thought and then write it down? No, no, said Feynman, (paraphrased). The *writing* is the *thought*.

Many times we have intuitions and half-formed hypotheses that only can be clarified by the clear statement and examination of them which writing allows. My hope has been that the writing of this book would drive me toward fresh insights. I believe it has.

Also, in our daily lives we are often constrained by social situations, mores, politeness, time limitations, verbal dexterity, complexity of subject, the glazed eyes of our audience, and numerous other factors from saying exactly what we believe to be the case. Right or wrong, a book is a wonderful place to say: Here it is! This is what I believe to be true.

The Brain

The brain is a **memory prediction** device. (Hawkins) A lot of the time consciousness is just along for the ride. Like the CEO of a large corporation, you (consciousness) are called upon many times only when there is a problem, only when the predictions of all the unconscious and automatic parts of the brain are not correct. This automatic, intuitive system of the brain scans the environment constantly attempting to make sense of the perceptions you have. Predictions can be mundane and ordinary. When you take a step in your living room, and your foot does not land on flat ground as you would expect, but on something in your path, this is an unexpected event, and your consciousness takes over, you look down and see a kid's toy.

Memory is associative. Associations can be causal, contiguous in space or time, or relations of meaning. Associations should be at least somewhat predictive.

Memory use is analogical. When we wonder how to react to a certain situation, our mind automatically searches our memory for similar situations and the way we reacted then and the outcome. The situations are never completely identical, and at times not even that similar, but may still contain enough resemblances to be useful. The development of memory use, as opposed to rigid instinctual behavior, was a major evolutionary advance. Douglas Hofstadter, an expert on analogy, has made the point that we utilize our memories to form categories or concepts analogically, as well.

The brain is more like a multi-purpose than single use tool, with many, many modules that do things below the level of consciousness and others at the conscious level. But though the brain is modular in the sense that different parts do different things, there is massive interconnectedness and interdependence between all parts. My focus here is on the general way the brain works as it applies to and constrains the workings of the mind.

The brain creates models of reality, beginning with your senses. (Hawkins, Hawking, others) The senses are as much constructions as reality, though most of the time they give you, for practical purposes, a fairly accurate portrayal of what is going on. Otherwise, our species would never have made it this far, and you and I would not be here. We make plans, mini-plans even, from the time we wake till we sleep again. On a typical morning, I rise, go into the living room to flip the computer on, back into the kitchen to start coffee making, into the bath to brush my teeth, and then return to the bedroom again to straighten my inevitable mess. This order of events allows the computer to warm up and the coffee to brew while I attend to these other things. Life is full of these mini-plans that involve our models of the world. My models contain small errors many times: I wake, plan to go to the health food store to pick up supplements, then suddenly realize it's Sunday and they are closed. These small plans seem mundane and somewhat boring, but the fact is they are the basis of all the larger ones. Our models of the world are complex and multi-faceted but they are based on the simple; and voluntary movement is where thoughts become material.

Consciousness allows us to sustain a thought or scenario in working memory and direct our thoughts. These activities are largely controlled by the frontal lobes, which not coincidentally, also control voluntary movement.

Many confusions center upon different conceptions of consciousness. Defining terms is always a good place to start. It should be noted that this use of definition is not completely rigid and rule-based, but deals with the typical. The major purpose of delineating terms is to make clear what aspect or concept is under discussion. **Consciousness can be defined as awareness, alertness, the attending to what is around you**. In this sense, most animals are conscious to some degree. This could be termed core consciousness. **In humans, however, there is a second level of awareness: we are aware that we are aware, conscious of being conscious. We know that we know**. This extended consciousness includes autobiographical memory and the ability to plan. I personally believe that much of this comes from our ability to use language to represent the world. A good analogy would be stereovision. Our feeling of depth perception comes from the two slightly different views our eyes give us. In the same way, we are able to compare our perceptions (imagistic concepts) with linguistic concepts present in our minds. There is what is happening around us, and the relevant memories that we bring forth and the stories we tell. These interact to produce a kind of depth perception of awareness.

In his landmark book on consciousness, Stanislaus Dehaene gives what is a key feature of science: an operational definition. **An operational definition can be measured and tested in some manner to see if a phenomenon is present**. He distinguishes consciousness from vigilance, awareness, and attention. Part of attention is unaware, he notes, so consciousness cannot be the same as attention, although often-times deliberate attention is necessary. Many times, however, our attention is not under conscious command. Think of how you react when you hear a sudden noise. If all our attending processes were conscious, we would face an infinite regress. Consciousness is consciousness of some object, for Dehaene. And consciousness of an object can be tested for and experimented with in many laboratories these days. Of special significance are objects at the very edge of awareness due to our processing speed, where approximately half the time you become conscious of them and the other half not. This makes consciousness a variable that can be identified and controlled. **This allows another keynote of scientific research: the experiment.** Dehaene and team have found 4 signatures of consciousness in the brain that tell us *when* consciousness of some object is present. Sudden activation of the parietal and frontal lobes, then a long, slow negative wave, followed by bursts of high-frequency gamma activity, and finally global exchange of synchronized signals, together indicate consciousness is present. For much more detailed and precise discussion and definitions of these markers, see his work, *Consciousness and the Brain.*

There is no need for the hypothesis of a language of thought. **Thought is based on our perceptions of our own body and actions, and those of the objects and events around us in the world. Intelligence begins in the body.** Thoughts are mental representations but not necessarily, or even usually, in linguistic form. This is true historically also. Of course, if you *define* thought as a linguistic structure with an object and action then thought is linguistic. But most people (and certainly not animals), do not think this way, all or even perhaps most of the time. They think in sensory images of one type or another. Think about the way you think (which is metacognition) as you move through the day. Is it in images? Words? I am language-oriented and find, many times, I am carrying on an internal dialogue during daily activities. However, much of the time I am enjoying the input of my senses: the sights and sounds, the feel of the breeze, and my thoughts consist of sensory images. Or studying a chessboard, simulating a position as it will look after a few more moves. Thoughts come in different shapes and varieties. In accord with the ideas of embodied cognition, *Louder Than Words* by Benjamin Bergen has outlined different experiments which show that humans create visual images for many sentences that we hear and read, in order to understand them. The internal dialogue of our thinking is represented by auditory images.

And another groundbreaking book, *The Ghost In My Brain,* details how disruptions in vision and the spatial sense can make cognition and everyday life incredibly difficult. The author, Elliot Clark, had a concussion and suffered disruptions in his thought processes for years, until neuroscientific therapy and pioneering work with specially made glasses utilized paths of the optic nerves that had been previously idle and were undamaged. So the popular earlier idea of thought as computation, detached from the body, completely rational and austere, has been largely replaced, or at least augmented, by a more physical, body-oriented view. **Thought begins with our perceptions of our bodies and environment.**

You could reserve the word thought for these linguistic structures, and use cognition as the word for broader aspects: perception, attention, memory, learning, etc., and this path has obviously been taken by some. **This points again to that major problem in the study of many complicated subjects: definition of terms.** Many times there are major philosophical or scientific arguments caused by the use of the same term in different ways by different people. The concept of consciousness is one good example of this. The concept of intelligence is another.

The idea of the mind as having the primary function of acquiring, encoding, storing, and retrieving information strikes me as important and valid, and fits into the framework of a memory prediction network, as long as we realize that this is not meant to be solely the manipulation of symbols but is based on the world we interact with and evolved in. Information is a valuable concept which cuts across many disciplines.

If true artificial intelligence is to be developed, and I believe it will be, it most likely will come by hooking up inputs and outputs from the real world to a computer (robot) and in some fashion allowing it to learn from interactions with its environment through sensors. Although it is hard to see what exactly could be at stake for such a machine, unless it is survival, as survival is for us. Our faculties and intellect have been shaped and honed by evolutionary forces and time. This "aboutness" defines the process of thinking. Perhaps some recognition of the difference between good (favorable) and that of bad (unfavorable) environments, and preference for the former could be instilled. I have envisioned artificial intelligence mostly optimistically and also have no doubt that the combinatorial fusions of technology and the human body will continue to increase, as they have already proliferated to create: the blind seeing again, better and smaller hearing devices, prosthetics of all types, and possible recovery from spinal injuries. The notion of a cyborg becomes ever more realistic and possible. One of the many interesting ideas put forth by physicist David Deutsch is that technology and science have no intrinsic limits except those decreed by the laws of nature. Basically, that given enough time and knowledge, almost anything can be accomplished. I must agree. The billion-dollar question is whether our species will survive long enough to realize those potentials.

Others have envisioned the rise of artificial intelligence more darkly, seeing in it our inevitable replacements. Again, my vision is of a more symbiotic nature.

Although the main focus of this work is definitely **not** on the physical parts of the brain, but about its functions at the more abstract level of mind, it may be useful to the reader for us to take a brief, brief tour of the major brain areas and their functions.

Major

Brain Areas

Some major parts of the brain and their functions:

Hippocampus

Involved in the formation of memories, especially spatial memories. Without a properly functioning hippocampus, new memories cannot be laid down.

Frontal Lobes

The seat of the executive function of the brain. Involved in thought and planning, and as a consequence, in voluntary movement. A central way station in the interconnections of the brain.

Parietal Lobes

Involved in spatial activities. The "where" part of the visual pathway. Receives and integrates sensory information.

Temporal Lobes

Heavily involved with language production and reception. Also, the rear of the temporal is involved with object recognition. The medial temporal lobe has structures necessary for long term memory formation and storage.

Occipital Lobe

The vision section of the brain, which is divided into areas of increasing complexity and abstraction as what is seen is processed.

Sensory Strip

A strip along the mid cortex with areas leading to the major sensory part of the body, with the size of the area proportionate to the sensors involved.

Motor Strip

An area in the rear of the frontal lobe that contains sensors to the various body regions and helps to plan and control movements.

Cerebellum

The cerebellum is crucially involved with coordination, balance, control, and timing of movements.

Cerebral cortex

The layered gray matter of the brain where thought, attention, perception are processed. Processes input and, at the same time, relays feedback from the brain memory areas, so that input is modified by prior experience.

Thalamus

A central way station through which many pathways from other different areas pass. Helps regulate attention, consciousness, and alertness.

Neurons

The nerve cells of the brain and nervous system that process and transmit information through electrical and chemical means. Neurons fire in groups or networks.

Amygdala

Involved in memory consolidation and emotions.

Intelligence

A good general definition of intelligence **is the ability to solve problems and reach goals by overcoming obstacles.** An appropriate definition for our purposes might include the capacity to reason by forming, manipulating and combining concepts and symbols for thoughts and language.

But intelligence is a construct. **A construct is a concept which is posited to aid in explanation but has no actual physical reality.** Therefore, these concepts are subject to different interpretations and there have been many, many definitions of intelligence proposed. The situation is reminiscent of Humpty Dumpty in *Through the Looking Glass* who says a word can mean whatever he wants it to.

Most of these definitions mention some combination of perception, learning, concept formation, consciousness, thought, symbolic understanding and manipulation, volition, reasoning ability, pattern recognition, and/or problem solving, in one fashion or another.

My belief is that perception and concept formation are the basis of all the other mental activities. If you didn't have concepts, reality would only be the "blooming, buzzing confusion" so often mentioned, and the evidence is that children start out with a small (though important and essential) core group of concepts at birth, and only gradually learn the multitudes they eventually attain as adult human beings. (Carey) **Although the distinction between perception and concepts is valid, and having perceptions without concepts is possible, it is not usual, and for most practical purposes perception *is* perception of concepts.** As normal human beings moving through our days and lives, we perceive that around us in terms of its conceptual meaning. Another form of this point should be made concerning conscious and unconscious thought. Thought is based in, and is part and parcel of, perception. We have signals flowing from our senses into the brain, and immediate feedback from the brain as it makes meaning of them. This is not what philosophers usually are referring to. They prefer to focus on conscious rational thought, drawing a sharp line between "sensing" and "thinking." The contrast between feeling the warmth of the sun, and thinking about the warmth, which can be carried out without sensory input. And this distinction does help contrast perception and thought, though it is misleading, since there is no actual separation between the two; and perception is the basis and beginning of conceptual understanding and thought, not only in humans, but perhaps most other living creatures. Our perceptions normally consist of concepts and combinations of them in interaction. We don't just see bright lights and a rectangular shape coming at us: we see a car. We don't just see rectangular blocks on a street, we see houses. Or elongated shapes walking upright, we see people. As I jog through my neighborhood, I view houses, cars, trees, people, animals, and many other objects; I hear the leaves rustle, feel the breeze and smell the new-mown grass. And when I spot movement ahead of me, my first thought (although almost always unstated linguistically) usually is, "what is that?" Is it a dog, or a cat, perhaps a raccoon, or just a plastic bag swirling in the wind? Because my actions might be different according to that identification: especially when it is, in fact, a dog. And this is common for humans as we scan our environment, gauging the flow of entities and actions occurring around us, and what they might mean. When you enter a well-known environment—your office, for example—you might not think about what all the objects are because they are familiar and part of your background knowledge. But in a strange alley at midnight, you are likely alert to every subtle change in sound, odor, and nuance of sight, stretching your senses to identify the various elements and make conceptual meaning of your surroundings.

That is one reason definition is so important. The major terms in this text have been defined so as to illuminate the sense of the concept that is being used. We can only **understand** each other if our meanings are clear. This, again, is not rigid, rule-based definition, but sufficient delineation of a concept to distinguish it from others. And the giving of a physical basis to a construct, which we shall see later with the very *concept* of concept itself, removes it from the completely abstract realm into that of the physical world, and makes it subject to scientific discussion and experiment.

Understanding, as pointed out by Susan Greenfield in *Mind Change*, has to do with relating things or events to each other. *Related to this idea* is that science concerns the formation of concepts and their linkages. The word itself had always puzzled me. I had never completely "understood" the significance of "standing beneath." But, originally, the etymology shows, understanding often meant "standing among or between." Which seemed much more apt. Understanding has to do with *relationships.* We each have a model of the world that grows and changes as we do, and the more complex and accurate and complete that model is, the better our *understanding*. The more numerous and accurate connections that our model contains, the closer we are to understanding. This fits into the idea of crystallized intelligence, in which we use our knowledge and experience to make decisions. This type of intelligence grows throughout most of our lifespan. Fluid intelligence, on the other hand, is the raw ability to solve novel problems, as used by Greenfield. Flynn's distinction seems somewhat different, since he attributes a large part of the IQ gains in this past century to a cultural milieu in which abstract scientific thought has become much more pervasive, and calls this gain a gain in fluid intelligence.

Flynn's criteria for intelligence in *What Is Intelligence?* include mental acuity, knowledge and information, attitudes, habits of mind, memory, and processing speed. As an older person whose processing speed has decreased, I believe the actual *grasping* of the material is more vital than the speed, though it may be a good indication of general mental ability.

Also mentioned by many as factors of modernity are the rise of the use of abstraction, the detachment of logic and the hypothetical from the concrete. These are modes of thought that came into being with literacy, and became more widespread in the modern scientific world, especially by formation of the educational systems we now have. We tend to take this background for granted, but it certainly was not always thus. A mere six or seven hundred years ago, none of that was part of daily life. Even a hundred years ago, the educational system taught in a much different fashion, reached a much lower percentage of the population for less time, and was archaic, compared to the modern time's longer, much more intense experience. Literacy was the prerequisite for this process that has changed the shape of our world. Personal habits and exercises naturally do also strengthen mental abilities. Writing, reading, crossword puzzles, brain teasers, chess, and serious study of difficult subjects are all of value, especially the last.

The modern education has increased in both depth and breadth, with many advanced subjects now taught in addition to the areas of basic knowledge. Although it is not impossible to gain knowledge on your own, it can be more difficult. Guides have been useful in straying from the trodden paths, but independent exploration is valuable, as well. One advantage of independent study is the ability to pursue exactly the subjects you desire.

So, many and various qualities have been postulated as making up intelligence, but these above certainly seem apt and fairly comprehensive. Most of the factors listed are vital to creating an accurate and complete model of the world, and detailing the connections between the various parts of that model. To have that good model, that *understanding*, and to actively *utilize* it, would seem to me to be the beginnings of wisdom.

Emotional Intelligence has also been studied. At its roots emotion is either a positive or aversive reaction to an entity or situation. There are many degrees of variation in those reactions, from love to hate and everything in between. It has been found that in decisions where large numbers of variables are involved, your "gut" instinct is often more accurate than your conscious evaluations. It has been speculated that this is because your unconscious developed with the ability to take in large numbers of factors quickly in making decisions, and that your conscious mind may tend to weigh the most salient variables too heavily. People who sustain damage to the emotional centers of the brain find it difficult to make even simple decisions. Emotions are vitally involved in our thinking, which makes sense. Most events (I would say all) in our lives carry some sort of emotional overtones and people are vitally invested in making decisions which will affect themselves in positive ways. Although many times this is a battle of balance between long-term goals and immediate gratification.

Social Intelligence has also been much discussed, and has certainly been one driving force of our evolution. Primates are a gregarious and social lot. It has been speculated that the ability to function in groups, understanding others' points of view, motivations, and feelings (mindreading), was perhaps *the* main driving force for human intelligence. Autism has been associated with a sort of lack of social intelligence. People on the autistic spectrum many times have problems reading facial expressions and body language. You often learn more about a person from the way they move and talk and act then by the actual content of their conversation. I suspect that our symbolic capabilities may have diminished these abilities somewhat, as we came to rely on our symbolic worlds, and certainly some animals seem to read emotion and body language well.

Multiple other types of intelligence have been proposed, such as physical, musical, interpersonal, spatial, etcetera, notably by Howard Gardner, for one.

And, except for the very first general definition, these prior definitions of intelligence are largely anthropocentric. Science has come to realize that many animals show different types of intelligence to solve problems and cope with their worlds.

We could go on listing definitions of intelligence that highlight various facets of this concept, but I believe the point has been made and these should suffice.

Working memory function and capacity are also highly correlated with human intelligence. The two most vivid forms of working memory are mental images, also called a visuospatial sketchpad, and snatches of inner speech, called a phonological loop. (Baddeley and Hitch) Our experience is a mixture of perception and working memory. Even for long-term memories this is true. They need to be moved to working memory for use. One difference between humans and computers is that computers store each memory at a specific address. We humans use context and association as memory cues. This makes our memories harder to reach, many times, when these cues are absent. Language aids this with associative cues.

Concepts

For our purposes here, concepts are mental representations of categories. A category is a class of objects, events, actions, states, or mental constructs of some type. Concepts are not based on language but prior to language. They are the way we identify objects and creatures to interact with them in the world. They are the building blocks of thought. **Language allows us to label concepts, which makes them easier to recover from memory, combine, and manipulate.** It also allows us to build more complex concepts and linkages. **Concepts were based on similarity and resemblance originally**. (Foucault; Berman) In fact, before the advent of literacy, which itself brought forth a new way of thinking, there was not much, if any, formal analytical thought. **Thinking was based on resemblance, and metaphor was the natural result of this.** (Foucault) Although the typical philosophical discussion gets bogged down with the question of what exactly similarity consists of, I believe we know and recognize it quite well, most of the time. The classical (rule and definition based) concept more or less came into being with literacy. Before writing, the word and language were ephemeral. They were spoken, and then vanished. The written word allowed treating concepts as objects, with permanence, and permitted the building of much more elaborate structures of thought. (Ong) Thought could build upon thought, and be stored in external memory. A structure containing more abstract, formal concepts could be erected on top of those basic items dealt with every day. Though even common, everyday concepts are abstractions formed by our senses from our experience.

If you think of the universe as a huge pie, there are likely an almost infinite number of possible ways to slice that pie. Many might be uninteresting or unproductive, but among those would likely be a number of hidden gems which could illuminate some aspect of reality. (A quick note on infinity: I have never seen any real physical object which is infinite and believe this concept to be an informative and useful construct. See glossary for explanation of construct.) Here are some hopefully productive ways to consider concepts:

You could divide concepts into two broad classes, **1. Natural kinds,** or the fuzzy-edged type we get from clusters

of correlations in the real world. **Example**s: cat, horse, man, car, game.
2. **Classical, or rule based concepts**, the kinds made from definitions with rules, and necessary and sufficient conditions, the sharp-edged in or out type. Mathematical concepts, such as odd number, are classical. But even these have been shown to have members who are more typical than others. 3 as an example of an odd number is more salient than 237 for most people. The major theories of concepts either put forth the idea that we learn them from examples, the idea that we have a prototypical view of a concept in our mind (a bird has wings, a beak, feathers, two skinny legs, flies, lays eggs, etc.) that guides us when we meet a possible new instance of a concept, or the idea that we use all of our knowledge when we form a new concept, and assimilate it into our models of the world. I believe the truth to be a combination of these, with the idea that we use our knowledge

(including examples and prototypes) to fit a new concept into our existent models of the world in some way being primary.

Concepts may have many functions, but two of the main are reference and inference. When we categorize something, we can point it out, if it is material and in our vicinity, and we can infer certain things because of the category we have put it into. To repeat, concepts would be prior to language and based on interactions with the world. They are the way we generalize and simplify the world to deal with it, and they are the bridge between our thought and language. Concepts turn the world from a place with almost infinite individual numbers of objects into one with a much smaller number of types or kinds of things: objects, creatures, states, and events. Having its base in the physical world is what gives our language its power. Without this base, you are caught in the deconstructionist nightmare of an endless cycle of relationships which have no basis. Fortunately, this is not the case. Putting an object, action, event, or state in the proper category is a key step in thinking.

The basic level concept is a concept at a level with which we usually interact physically and constantly: car, boy, dog, cat, house, etc.

And these types of concepts are characterized by similarity of physical appearance and qualities. It has been said they combine distinctiveness (from competing concepts) and informativeness. (Murphy) Cats are easy to identify, and seeing that something is a cat allows you to infer a wealth of information about it. It purrs, has fur, likely hunts rodents or birds, does not always play well with dogs, is a carnivore, has excellent night vision, etc.

Superordinate concepts are more abstract, and group items that are often different and varied: vehicle, human, mammal, animal, building. And of course, a single object may be a member of many different categories, depending upon the purpose of the categorizer. I am a man, a husband, a father, a proud grandfather, mountain hiker, a chess player, a motorcyclist, a novelist, senior citizen, the turkey sandwich on table 12, and so on.

Subordinate concepts are more specific, and often used by experts, who tend to make finer distinctions in their fields of expertise: **jet plane, Homo sapiens, racing car.**

Philosophers sometimes divide the concepts in language into the relationship of reference that they have with the world, and the relationship, or sense, that they share with each other. The first is often ignored by those of deconstructionist bent.

There are many excellent and informative entire books written on the subject of concepts, from their origin to combination to the different theories explaining them. *The Origin of Concepts* by Susan Carey and *The Big Book Of Concepts* by Gregory Murphy are two. *Furnishing the Mind* by Jesse Prinz is another.

Quinian bootstrapping outlines a process used to learn new conceptual systems, described by Susan Carey. First, a group of new concepts are matched to objects or other concepts in a "placeholder" process: i.e. 1,2,3,4, to the equivalent groups of objects. Children learn to make this matching process without a real understanding why, by rote. But gradually they begin to map the correspondences between the numbers and sets of objects and understand their meaning.

The same process was used in teaching apes symbolic meaning. (Deacon) First they learned symbols that meant different individual foods (carrot, apple, orange, etc.) and individual tools (hammer, screwdriver, pliers, etc.). Then they learned symbols that generalized to each; i.e.: "food" and "tool", by repetition, and gradually came to understand (fit items into the proper categories) using those abstractions. This must have also been the manner in which the first human language learners learned, by naming individual objects and events, associating each with a particular sound or gesture, then only likely much later forming generalizations of these. This process appears to be an inductive one, where similarities in the objects under examination become apparent, the crucial insight is made, and a rule is formed. (Hey! You eat all these!)

This first learning process noted above, where the apes learned to associate individual items with symbols, was merely associative (or in Deacon's language, indexical). But the next two stages of the process, where the apes generalized to new symbols which indicated either the broader categories food or tools, and then, finally, were able to fit new instances into those categories, were truly symbolic. The apes had moved from associating signs and particular items to a system where logical relationships existed between the symbols themselves. This is the key step in having a true symbol system. If you add verbs to this system of signs, you are on your way to syntax and language. And learners view these categories as action placeholders, anyway, as humans and primates both likely tend to think of the objects of the world according to the ways in which they use them, as systems of affordances, not as objects-in-themselves.

This manner of learning new concepts as placeholders - then filling in those " skeletal sketches" with meaning gradually as the new system is learned or created, (as in the number system, noted by Carey and others) is evident in examples of conceptual change in scientific theorizing. The corresponding symbolic realization in learning the natural number system would be that each new number denotes a group of objects which is increasing by one, regardless of the type of object in the group.

Children go through the same type of inductive clue game when learning concepts. They are given the label ball for that round object they roll upon the floor, then point to the moon and call it ball also, and perhaps to a coin, because of its roundness, before they learn from trial and error what the defining characteristics of that particular category is. They over-generalize in this way (calling all animals dogs, for example,) or perhaps under-generalize, thinking cat is only the label for Fluffy over there in the corner, not all those purring, leg-rubbing creatures. This common conceptual learning is fairly obvious, however, compared to Newton's realization that the apple falling and the gibbous moon hanging up high above in the sky were, for certain purposes, the same kinds of objects and could be described as belonging to the same abstract category: as entities subject to gravity. But the difference in the conceptual process is more one of degree than kind.

Concepts can also be organized into: Kinds of, **Parts of**, **Instances of.** Kinds-of and parts-of hierarchies are fundamental to the organization of conceptual systems, and also involve rules that can contribute to explanation. Things that have the same types of parts are organized the same way and are usually the same kinds**.** (Thagard) If something has wings and feathers, it is likely a bird.

Types of conceptual change (Note: Several of these categories follow Thagard's distinctions.)

Distinction Learning is observed in many animals, where they learn to distinguish between two states or different types of objects or animals. This does not mean they have an abstract idea of the concept, though some primates and a few other animals undoubtedly do. In Ayn Rand's terms, this would be differentiation, which is followed by the integration of similars into categories, by the process of measurement omission. (Similars have the same qualities, but different measures.)

Coalescence: The joining of two concepts that were separate prior into one inclusive category. Darwin classified humans as animals in his theory, when before they had been considered a different and unique type of being. Copernicus reclassified the earth as a type of planet when it had been considered sui generis. Abstraction into superordinate categories is a kind of coalescence. Not dining room chair and living room sofa, but furniture. Not cars and boats and bicycles, but vehicles. Notice that this type of categorization allows you to highlight common aspects of entities which may seem superficially different. This is very common and useful in scientific theorizing. Maxwell joined not only electricity and magnetism to make one phenomenon (electromagnetism), but also discovered that light was an electromagnetic wave as well.

Differentiation: Dividing elements of one concept into several. The general concept heat became differentiated into two distinct concepts, heat and temperature. The general category fish differentiated when some fish were discovered to actually be mammals. Those bright shining objects in the night sky differentiated when some, the planets, were discovered not to be stars, but much closer, and to revolve around our own star.

Composition: Concepts may change in composition as discoveries are made, and new elements are found, as in subatomic particles in the atom. Or the discovery that water is actually a molecule made up of hydrogen and oxygen.

Creation: Original categories formed either by taking instances from other categories, discovering new commonalities, or creative thought. Concept combination is a form of new category creation: pet fish, sliding glass door, calendar girl, web site, comedy drama, etc. These new categories don't always follow simple rules of combination but combine in new and creative ways.

Complex concepts that organize groups of simpler ones are sometimes called **frames**. Just as simple concepts reduce the almost infinite variety of the world by generalization, frames group simple concepts together to form more complex concepts, under organizing principles. The frame for restaurant, for example, would include eating out, money passing hands in exchange for the meal, a server, tipping, a menu from which to order, etc. We have frames for almost every common event or institution in society. The protocols involved in a wedding, a football game, and a funeral are very different. You likely won't hear much loud laughter or cheering at a funeral, or see that much kissing either.

The term **frame** is also sometimes used to denote a particular way of presenting an event or situation, according to need. My charming wit may be your offensive sarcasm. My prudence might be your cowardice, your logic chopping my rigorous thought and so on. Everybody tends to frame events in ways which are suitable to their own purposes. Humans all have a horse in the race or a finger in the pie. We quickly peruse events around us to determine how they will affect us.

A **script**, on the other hand, is a group of concepts which follow each other like steps, or directions of an algorithm. Taking the prototypical restaurant example, again: being seated, given menus, ordering, eating, paying, leaving. Much of the time during conversation or written communication, however, the vast majority of what is communicated remains implicit, unstated, in the background. This vast store of background knowledge that most of us share is one reason it is so difficult to create artificial intelligence.

Many times, confusions about relationships or functions of concepts occur when one of the concepts is vague, imprecise, or incorrect. This can cause misunderstandings, since understanding involves concepts and the relationships they have to each other. Science, many times involves replacing a vague and general concept, like heat, with one that is precise and measurable, like temperature. Or by refining, through discovery, precisely what a concept is.

If a concept is a mental representation of a category, then would that mean that every different part of that category is represented or that only the specific part that is called for in a function? For example, when you have the concept dog you could have a visual image of a dog, also an audible one of a bark, perhaps memories of specific dogs, and facts that you know about dogs: that they have fur, four legs, are mammals, a domesticated species of wolf bred by man, make great pets, bark, etc. The fact that dogs are mammals is a good example of modern scientific formal thought. Classifying different animals as one group, though they vary widely, by being warm-blooded, and bearing their young live at birth, having fur or hair, etc., makes for a category with members that oral, or prescientific societies, would not have thought to lump together. Oral societies have a problem seeing the efficacy of such groupings, many times.

The specific representation that would be called up in any given context would be the concept tokened at that time in working memory, though all would likely be activated to some small unconscious extent, through association. Prinz, in *The Furnishing of the Mind*, calls this portion of the concept tokened a proxytype. It could be imaged and identified, in theory. The interesting thing about that, whether you term this a concept or proxytype, is that identifying it with a brain state turns it from a construct to a concept with a basis in reality. A few simpler concepts have already been identified by using imaging technology in practice. The various tokens of a concept would likely be stored in different brain areas, perhaps brought together in a convergence zone as per Antonio Damasio, in *The Feeling of What Happens.*

Concepts start in interactions with the world, and language is grounded out in the world. Although some concepts appear present at birth in infants and a core group are doubtless innate, the womb is the first environment, and the experience of the body in that environment may provide the beginnings of certain concepts. If we look back in evolutionary time, development was moderated by the environment from the beginning. If crystallized intelligence is a good term for the knowledge we acquire during our lifetimes, it is likely even more apt for our genetic, natural inheritance, which is crystallized intelligence of another sort. Life is an endless dance between organisms and environment.

Language no doubt began with words for objects and simple actions and terms like this and that for pointing at things and grew in complexity from those beginnings. Etymology, or the study of word history and origins, almost always finds the roots of language in the physical. This is what Postmodern and Deconstructionist type thinkers sometimes forget. Names and many other words are tied to the world by the act of pointing (reference), not by definition. (Pinker)

I have emphasized the point before in fictive form (see my novels *Sign Changes* and *Sign Journeys*) that much of what makes us human comes from our ability to understand and use symbols. Also, that the ways we use these symbols have changed our modes of thought. A brief overview of the major developments and changes caused:

Speech

Speech expanded our abilities to label, refine, communicate, and store concepts, thus allowing us to access them more easily. Also, greatly increased our abilities to think about events and items not in our immediate temporal and spatial vicinity. In my opinion, this was a key step in the enhancement of our capacity to imagine, to plan. To travel in time in our minds. To run simulations of possible futures without committing the actual necessarily somewhat risky acts. A number of current scientists believe this (imagination) to be the key ability that sets humans apart from the rest of creation. Without language, this could be likened to looking through a huge pile of material scattered haphazardly, here and there, in our memories. Language, like the organization of a filing cabinet, gave us much easier access to particular memories through association. Remember that day in October, in Redwood City, when the gorilla adopted the kittens? Of course you do. Language allows us to note and zoom in on the particular, though of course we conceptualize through generalization.

Literacy

Reading and writing made the word an object with permanency, one that could be viewed and manipulated into complex chains of reason or mathematical thought. Oral culture was largely constrained by the limitations of memory, but written culture gave us the foundations of possibility for modern science, formal analysis, of course, and basically many of the other building blocks of the world we live in today.

Literacy gave us a platform from which to develop abstract thought. Again, the written word allowed treating languages as objects with permanency, permitted the erection of more complicated structures of thought, and gave us external memory storage. And fostered uniformity and complexity of concepts, as well. The formal operations that characterize the modern world largely began with literacy. The abstract characterizations, classifications, and concept uniformity that science relies on. To entertain abstract thought, a hierarchy of concepts had to be built upon the concrete objects and events we see and sense every day. Structures of classification had to be erected, like that by Linnaeus, the father of modern taxonomy, a process of conceptual growth that continues even today. Witness the number of specialty fields in science now. Or even the number of cable television channels. We continue to increase and refine categories.

Formal Thought/Computers

The computer is the culmination of the era of formal thought that literacy and scientific reasoning fostered. I will not delve here into all the possible changes in modes of thought that computers have brought about. They are varied and complex and beyond the scope and purpose of this work. Not only that, we are still in the infancy of the computer age, and like those in the midst of any revolution, it is difficult to grasp its significance completely. A book could be written about this subject alone, and many have been.

This era began with the realization that symbols were just that: symbols, and could take on any meaning desired. This fostered formal thought: logic, abstract art, free verse, scientific reason. The computer builds that realization from a foundation using only the symbols 0 and 1 to construct … anything. Well, almost anything, theoretically, and one possibility that will likely be realized is…

Artificial Intelligence

My feeling again is that this will come about by developing true intelligence, that is, intelligence with the ability to learn from its environment. This will likely be an organic process, where the intelligence "develops by feedback" from the world. Perhaps fostered on something similar to the way the neurons in the brain "fire together, wire together" to map reality. Sensory inputs of some types similar to ours would be a vital part of this process, allowing comparisons of data and sensory information. As also mentioned prior, I believe that these symbolic comparisons to sensory are likely a necessary part of the development of our type of consciousness.

Korzybski's famous dictum should be remembered, however: that the map is not the territory. The word spoken is never the thing itself. The description is never the actuality.

But this *is* one reason language is so endlessly useful. While it may never *be* the things it describes, its basis in the real world can help us envision and simulate alternate possible realities and our projected futures more accurately. Many times, in my opinion, the more concrete and simple the language, the closer the relationship to reality, though, as Einstein once warned, (paraphrased), make things as simple as possible, but no simpler.

In exception to this rule are a group of statements first introduced by J.L. Austin, called performatives, whose use actually creates a reality, though this reality is often psychological, ceremonial, or legal in nature. These are terms such as "I do" when spoken at a wedding, or oral acceptance of a contract, for example. The bailiff calling that the court is in session.

Also, the human race weaves narratives about anything and everything. We are storytelling creatures. And such tales tend to take on a certain reality of their own. Reality has an amorphous quality, and our stories help us give it form. Think of the countless narratives about the events of the past half century. There is no one single master narrative that is *the* story of those years. Instead, there are many. The same could be said for any event which involves many people: there may be a basic set of facts upon which there is agreement; (or perhaps not even that) but there will be as many narratives as humans. We each have a story to tell.

Language is the way we reach for reality, talk about it, but language never is what it describes. This endless back and forth between the wonderful variety of things language allows us to know and express, and the fact that it never quite touches reality is a paradox and tension that itself endlessly lurks in and informs my own writing. One of the marvelous things about good fiction is that it attempts to breach this existential gap by creating imagery in your mind, imagery that makes a virtual world real for a time.

But this linguistic paradox is only a reflection of a larger one, that of the split that occurred between humans and our world when rationality became a dominant mode of dealing with reality. Rationality creates and requires a distance from the world, an objectification. (Berman, Pirsig) And as Pirsig has remarked, nothing is ever gained without something else being lost. We are driven to think, but sometimes just long for that feeling of oneness with our surroundings and the earth that has been lost living in symbolic worlds. That is one of the reasons I go to the mountains or watch a sunrise at the beach, and quiet all the questioning at times: to just *be*.

Symbolism

Gesture is the beginning of a system where one thing can mean another: it is an iconic precursor to symbolism and language. It is likely where language began. It is metaphorical in nature, and thus is also a bridge between the concrete and abstract... A communicative gesture isn't what it signifies, but often resembles it in some way.

Mirror neurons are active during gesture, are speculated to be in the speech centers of the brain, and are a possible indication that gesture was a precursor to speech. Cross-modal mappings would be a precursor to gesture. For example, the visual mapping and the body mapping of a primate swinging through trees. The motor map of an action and the visual map of seeing an action. The visual mapping and body mapping involved in imitation. Cross-modal mappings would also seem to be a precursor and analogue of metaphor.

Resemblance appears to be at the bottom of all of this in one form or another. Pattern recognition is the resemblance not only of things but of relationships between things, and relationships between relationships. We categorize based on resemblance, build metaphors based upon partial resemblance. Resemblance is the stepping stone between concrete and abstract thought. **We model systems by simplifying them and eliminating the**

nonessential resemblances and keeping the important. This is always true. A completely accurate model of something would be an exact duplicate of it, which due to the retention of all the complexity of the original is not usually useful. Why not use the original? The key is in knowing which elements are essential. **Computers have allowed us to run much more complex and accurate models.**

There is some evidence that the idea of the monolithic self is partially a symbolic illusion of sorts. Many writers, including Dennett, have noted the idea that the self is largely a story we tell ourselves, though if it is, it is one we believe deeply. Others have noted that the "self" is situational and changes according to role and association. My belief is the self, like language, is grounded in the physical body, which is the root of these other concepts of self. And that, yes, we use narrative to weave a coherent sense of self, which certainly can help account for some rather bizarre behavior at times, either due to the unreality, incoherence, or the breakdown of that narrative.

As noted prior, the key element in a symbol is that it means more than its physical presence; that it points to another part of the universe besides itself. Physical signs point in a direct and obvious way. The clouds signifying possible rain. The smoke from a fire. Symbols are often arbitrary, with meanings and linkages that are not obvious or deducible from their physical appearance, although as mentioned above, they may be iconic to reality in some ways. They probably came about by associations similar to that of the physical signs, however. A sound, or a gesture, perhaps, was linked with an object in the vicinity through repetition, and the sound or gesture came to "signify" that object. This is a marvelous and wonderful event, when you really think about it. One part of the universe linked to and meaning or signifying another. Which is really the catalyst or beginning of the idea of "meaning."

So, symbols became linked to meanings by way of association, as physical objects and events do. These linkages led to ideas of cause and effect, as well. This chain is obvious in all parts of life, and associations have led to false pairings, as in superstition, whereby the joining of action and event led ballplayers not to change their socks or shave, ladders not be walked under, and cracks on the sidewalk to be avoided in walking down the street. Or false cause and effect pairings have been postulated in science when two events or objects only are correlated, with perhaps a single underlying cause of both.

We are meaning-seeking creatures unlike any other that walks, swims, crawls, or flies on this planet. If something has no meaning, we are likely to create one. Witness the Rorschach inkblot test. Abstract art. Hallucinations of those who have been deprived of sensory input. Constellations in the nighttime sky. The human attribute of meaning-seeking takes us from the distorted depths of paranoia to the heights of genius.

We live in an increasingly abstract world of our own creation. Money has gone from being some portable object of value, to paper backed by valuable objects, to paper that is valuable only because we all agree it is, to electronic symbols. Even the idea of money was a great step forward in abstraction that grew from trading. This idea that objects may have meaning only by our agreement is very interesting, but at times such as financial crises, that agreement may break down.

There are financial investment instruments of a complexity and variety inconceivable a century ago. Specialty areas of science. Distinctions of types of sex and gender. Cable television channels and programs.

Expertise is an interesting concept. Experts make more numerous and finer distinctions in their particular areas of interest. Scientists are, of course, some of our most important experts, and the distinctions they make filter down eventually to the rest of society. We do, in fact, know more and more about less and less.

The act of making meaning may be endless and the highest act of creation. Creativity has been mistakenly believed to be the realization of a new idea, ex nihilo, from nothing. But we all stand on the shoulders of those who came before us, and any new idea is actually always built from what is already known, and is usually the linkage of two or more concepts that have never been joined in a particular way before, perhaps. One part of the universe pointing at another.

Metaphor

As used in this work, metaphor may be defined as the use of any word in a non-literal sense. Much of this discussion is based upon ideas first seen in Guy Deutscher's landmark book, *The Unfolding of Language.*

As stated above, concepts are the common ground of thought and language. If you trace almost any word back to its origins, they will be physical in nature. Metaphor is the main bridge between concrete language and abstract. Every metaphor is an implicit analogy.

An analogy compares the relationship between one thing and another to another relationship between two things or events. Her cheeks were red as fire compares the relationships between red and fire and red and her cheeks.

There are two major modes of thought: analogical and digital, iconic and symbolic. Metaphor is largely iconic.

We move from the concrete to the abstract, and metaphor is our main vehicle. Metaphor takes us from the physical realm into those of time, logic, and reason. (Natural language has almost unending layers of meaning. That is why it is so rich.) The exception to expansion by metaphor comes largely by superordinate concepts, in which we join items into larger and more abstract groups. These groupings also move us further away from the concrete and open up an aspect of creativity, as the objects of our groupings are always accessible to revision and necessity. Concepts like vehicle, which encompasses automobiles, boats, 4-wheelers, etc. The category *animals* includes many varieties of creature that often do not resemble each other at all. These types of abstractions group basic concepts that we usually already are familiar with, but combine them according to some type of new, different motif. Ad-hoc concepts like "things to take on a vacation trip" are good examples of dissimilar objects included under one "umbrella" concept. So the sheer expansion of the number and types of concept is one way we are able to think more abstractly. This process permits us to make larger, more inclusive generalizations. But metaphor is the actual *mechanism* by which we leave the physical. (And ubiquitous: Please note that mechanism itself is a metaphor when used in this sense. There is no actual physical mechanism being discussed here. Almost every sentence I see contains a metaphor of some type.)

Language is full of metaphors which we have forgotten are metaphors, (Deutscher) which came from the simplest physical relations. **Beside, in, before**, **at, from, behind, through, within, after, by, around**. First used for spatial relations, extended to time and many to reason or cause. Who is coming **beside** you? I will be there a**round** four. Solutions **within** reason. I will be there **by** three. Good, come **in** time.

Before originally meant to stand in front of, as in stand **before** you. Now, it is usually used in other, more abstract senses, as in be there **before** noon, in which the meaning has been extended to the sense of prior, or in front of, in a temporal way.

With has gone from signifying physical presence to the abstract: she moved **with** grace.

At the beach. **At** noon. **At** peace. From a physical place, to an abstract time, to an even more abstract state of mind.

This and **that** have been transferred from the spatial act of pointing to the abstract space of conversation. **This is what I'll do. That is the end of it.** Words like **go** and **have, though they still retain their original meanings,** have expanded them to include the abstract: **I'm going to do it. I have to do it.**

Like evolution, language is a tinkerer, and tends to work with what is already available, instead of reinventing the wheel: reusing the concrete, but expanding meaning to the abstract. We understand the abstract, many times, by understanding the physical first.

Language has many implicit conceptual metaphors, like TIME IS SPACE and EVENTS ARE OBJECTS; TO KNOW IS TO HAVE SOMETHING. George

Lakoff and Mark Turner brought the pervasiveness of these metaphors in daily language use to public attention in their pioneering work in *Metaphors We Live By.*

We tend to reference abstract entities by using the concrete. Seeing abstract objects as containers is another common metaphor: We will see you *in* May, as if the month of May was a physical container. We do this all the time without even thinking about it. Just a further quick illustration: the word "pioneering" in the paragraph above was originally used to denote foot soldiers in the army who went first and paved the way for the rest, then later came to signify physical explorers of new lands, and that sense carries over to the exploration of new topics, which is how I used the term. I could go through every sentence in this piece, and find hidden metaphors in almost all.

We represent time by spatial metaphors because time is abstract, and it helps us to think about it in a way that is understandable. Christmas is *ahead* of us. (Right around the corner.) The hard part is *behind* us. Summer is *almost on top of us*. My feeling is that the concept "time" doesn't really have an independent existence. What we *have* are events that follow each other. All the ways that we measure time actually are comparisons of types of events. The events are real, and time is a useful and informative concept in our daily lives, but is a construct in the sense discussed below. (See glossary for definitions of construct and reification). Events can be pointed at: time never can be. And events cannot be undone. That is why time travel (to the past, anyway) is not a real possibility, and space and time are forever intertwined**.**

If no events are occurring, is time passing? I stated once in a fictional work that if ever there was a time when there was truly nothing, then there still would be. Modern science concurs with this, using the uncertainty principle to show that the position and momentum of particles cannot both be zero at once. Thus, space is never truly completely empty.

Illusions have much to teach us about our thinking processes. Many illusions occur because our vision evolved in a three dimensional world, and the necessities of that do not always translate exactly to the two dimensional page. One of my favorite illusions is that of the picture in which you see either two faces in profile, at times, or the outline of a vase, but never both at the same instant. This is an interesting phenomenon in which the object of our attention remains the same, but our perception of it changes. These are called flipping illusions. This occurs because we evolved an ability to recognize objects, and when we find two conflicting objects (figure-ground conflict) in the same image, our brain oscillates between them. This dual image in one reminds me how many meanings can be contained in one word, and how those sometimes alternate in your mind as well, as pointed out by Richard Gregory in his excellent book on illusions, *Seeing Through Illusions*, about the dual meanings of the word "through" in the title. An astute reader may have noticed that the title of this work, *Mind Views*, has a dual meaning as well. This reminds us again how what we see is as much constructed by the brain as perceived, as Gregory and many others have noted.

Scientific Truth and Theory

Truth may be defined as a statement which points out a state of affairs that really does obtain in the world. This, broadly speaking, is known as the correspondence theory of truth.

A fact is a state of affairs in the world that actually exists and can be verified by repeated observations.

A scientific law is a description, usually mathematical, of the way things work. Though, as an amateur (and poor) student of mathematics at various times,

I think it must be pointed out that mathematical statements can always be translated into language and concepts we are familiar with, even if this is often laborious, tedious, and lengthy. There has been much debate and controversy about the exact ontological status of mathematics. I believe the generalization, precision, and abstraction of the concepts used in mathematics give it power to encompass almost any natural phenomenon and accounts for its endless uses. Quantification was one key to modern science. Mathematics, in a deep sense, is all about patterns. Pattern recognition is a key aspect of human cognition, and mathematics gives us one way to fit almost anything into some type of pattern or formula. Intelligence, concepts, symbols, metaphors, and theory could all be discussed in terms of pattern recognition. Which brings to mind our old friend "resemblance" once more.

Science proceeds by a process of Induction: Observing a finite number of examples and framing generalizations. The hidden premise of induction is that tomorrow will resemble today, and the rest of the universe resembles the part we live in. Although this is somewhat simplistic, as the conceptual framework of the explorers of the unknown is also always vital. This is like that cartoon where two scientists are looking at a long equation with the spot in the middle that says: **And then a miracle occurs**. Without the relevant conceptual framework, and some kind of analogical, abductive, or Bayesian leap, you can see unlimited numbers of examples of phenomena and never make the correct inductive generalizations.

A theory is generally a deeper and broader coherent explanation of scientific laws that makes testable predictions.

It is theory, theory, theory, all the way down. Our very perception is theory-ridden to accommodate the type of place we live in: a world with gravity, and light that shines from above. We have intuitive theories about physical objects, their states and movements; about animate objects (agents) and the different way *they* move, and about quantities and magnitudes. These theories reflect the environment that our species evolved in and dealt with.

A construct is an abstract concept that helps us explain some phenomenon. Examples would be such concepts as intelligence, mind, cognition, emotions, self, the unconscious. You can point to examples of intelligence, but never to intelligence itself. That is why so many definitions of abstract concepts sometime exist. **The treatment of these abstractions as if they were concrete objects is the error of reification.**

Constructs were defined by Cronbach and Meehi in 1955, and David Levy, in *Tools for Critical Thinking*, points out typical constructs and develops an argument for distinguishing two types of theory, Event Theory and Construct Theory. Event theories are those which can be verified by fact, concerning actual events. (Did an asteroid hit the earth 65 million years ago and cause a great die-off?) Construct theories are those which can never be verified–by their very nature–because they use constructs which cannot be checked for factual accuracy. They are conceptual frameworks explaining facts, but the framework itself is not factual in nature, but abstract, and is impossible to check or verify.

Examples of construct theory include the theories of gravity, magnetism, electricity, sound, light, and energy.

In *Cognition, Brain, and Consciousness*, **inferred concepts** are discussed. An inferred concept, the authors Bernard Baars and Nicole Gage say, is a concept that is firmly anchored in reliable observations, but in agreement with Levy, is a construct which is always somewhat tentative. Newton's and Einstein's different conceptions of gravity are given as examples. In another example, the sun, the planets, and force are noted as instances of inferred concepts. This leads to the conclusion that some concepts, such as those of the sun and planets, were first inferred as the types of entities science now knows they are without much direct evidence, and only later, due to better technology and the accumulation of knowledge about these bodies, became considered facts; while other concepts, such as force and gravity, can never be confirmed in this way, because they are abstractions, useful fictions of explanation. Force, mass, and acceleration were turned into precise and useful concepts by Newton, of course, with his famous formula *force = mass x acceleration.* Science depends on this constant process of inference leading from raw observations to explanatory concepts. These inferences are the other side of the "induction" coin. Observation is necessary but never sufficient; it must be joined with a useful conceptual framework to make scientific discoveries.

Another concept similar to these would be that of the atom, which started out as a theoretical construct that was unobservable, but later, due to advancements in technology, became observable and considered a reality, though our exact model of the atom changes as science advances.

So, there seem to be different classes of constructs here. Or, rather, more accurately, the possibility that some constructs may be verified by deeper observation, while others, due to their abstract nature, remain theoretical.

Those that can be verified are obviously physical in nature, entities many times: sun, planets, atom; although this distinction is often dependent on the technology available. Many constructs have been hypothesized in scientific history which have later been found to be nonexistent. Good examples would be the "ether" as a medium through which objects moved in space, and "phlogiston" as an element of combustion.

I agree with Levy and many others that some theories cannot be verified as factual. That is due to their very nature. General theories of how things work often proceed by taking a number of related or seemingly unrelated facts and tying them together in a theoretical (coherent set of explanatory statements) structure. By its very nature, this type of theory cannot be proven factual. The function of the theory is to tie facts or observations together. This binding, itself, cannot be factual. It is an explanation of the facts. Imagine that the multitudes of facts concerning the world are sewing needles with eyes, jutting up all over the earth. Theories would be the invisible threads that tie various sets of these facts together. The facts are verifiable. These types of theories are not.

So perhaps these construct theories cannot be truthful, in the sense of the word used above, but I am not convinced that pure utility is their only difference. My problem is that when examining Einstein's Theory of Gravity I cannot help but think it is not only more useful, but a better theory than Newton's. Why? Because it explains more. It allows a greater number of predictions and makes them in additional domains. The concept of gravity itself changes from that of a force to a geographical feature of space and time. **I cannot help feeling it is a**

more accurate theory, a closer approximation of the way things are. That it is progress in the scientific domain. That is my quandary. Einstein's Theory does not completely invalidate Newton's. It takes it as a subset in a limited domain. The question really is: are we coming closer and closer to an accurate description of reality, or are our theories simply more or less useful? This is an open question. Can we know reality? Perhaps knowing reality is similar to the way a "limit" works in calculus, where asymptotes and lines approach ever more closely, but never quite touch.

Scientific Laws are descriptions of regularities in the physical world. Theories are explanations of these laws. Truth is when a fact agrees with reality. By their very nature these theories cannot agree with reality as a fact does. They are explaining the facts that do so. They are at the next metaphysical level.

They can give more accurate predictions, explain more things, be more coherent, simple, elegant, parsimonious. They can be better explanations, as Deutsch and others have noted.

And of course these concepts and theories are always subject to revision as we learn more, just like any others. We may find new information about the sun's or a star's life cycle or its origin. Or our criteria may change, as in the recent demotion of Pluto from planet status. The idea of usefulness applies to constructs as well as theories: constructs are mini-theories.

In the instances up above of sun and planet the entity was not abstract, but its actual ontological status was in question. **The concept of concept itself could have been considered a construct, and has been by many, but basic concepts have now been instantiated in the brain**. Modern technology has identified some simpler concept images utilizing imaging equipment. The mapping has begun, if only in a crude and basic manner. These images of thoughts were so similar and consistent (to other images) when subjects were asked to imagine certain objects, that the object's identity could be deduced later by other people who only studied the images! Mind-reading, at least in a basic sense, has become a reality.

Someday we may be able to almost completely map brain states. Although no two will likely ever be completely identical due to the fact that people change incessantly and so does the outer environment. The river cannot be made to stand still.

Conclusion

Nearly 14 billion years ago, (13.8 according to latest estimates) our best theory tells us the universe burst into being during a singularity known as the big bang. All that we see and know came from that instant. We are connected–in fact, as well as desire–to everything that began its existence in that singularity. The evidence is that life began on this planet one time only, and so we are also connected to all other living beings on earth. Evolutionary evidence also points to the fact that every human alive today possesses mitochondrial DNA from one common woman ancestor who lived some 100,000 to 200,000 years ago. So we are connected in that way, as well.

Our minds are products of our brains. We use our memory of what has been to predict what will be, and to take us places far away in space and time from where we are. Our imaginings are built from these memories we have. People whose memories are damaged have problems imagining. Many have noted imagination may be our most valuable asset. The ability to simulate possible futures without actually performing the acts involved gave our species an incredible tool of survival.

Living entities all use concepts. A concept, for an entity, is a difference in the world that makes a difference to them. Concepts generalized the physical world, through resemblance, into a manageable number of entities we could deal with. Concepts are the lingua franca, the currency of thought. And, of course, we humans have more concepts and can make more distinctions than any other living beings we now know of.

Symbol use gave us a new and unprecedented ability to conceptualize and manipulate the world around us. Language took us places we had never been, to create new entities unseen and unthought prior. It allowed a profuse conceptual expansion in humanity: a leap that permitted creation of both problems and solutions never before dreamt of. Each major advance in our symbolic abilities, from gesture, to speech, to writing, to the present day formal thought of the scientific and computer age, has changed us in unpredictable and unforeseen ways. Plato bemoaned the loss of memory due to writing as others bemoan the loss of depth in thought now due to the style of skimming, surfing thought brought on by the modern day internet. From early unconscious use, to visual object of our language, to the formal realization of these modern times, our thought has echoed our conceptual development. It is no accident that the past century was the century of form, with the computer, free verse, abstract art, logic, and scientific reason all blossoming and becoming part of the common gestalt.

Along with symbol use came a new objectification of and distance from our world. As stated before in fictional work, we *literally* cannot imagine the total immersion of our ancestors in their world, and modern humans long for the return of that feeling sometimes without even knowing exactly what we are longing for.

Metaphor, along with the structures of superordinate and formal concepts, allowed us to move from concrete language, based upon the entities and

objects of the everyday world, into more abstract realms.

Formal science and the scientific method, which at its most basic involves testing our hypotheses against the real world, were of necessity preceded by literacy. Although we were likely almost always testing them practically and informally. Only the ability to see our words as objects, and to store them and manipulate them via the written page, gave our concepts the operational uniformity first needed for widespread formal abstract thought. This method made our testing of reality rigorous, falsifiable, and correctable, and permitted the growth of knowledge.

We are at the beginning of an era of great expansion of our knowledge of the brain, brought on in large part by machines and technologies which allow us to image that organ. There should be more emphasis placed in our educational programs on the nature of thought, concepts, symbols, and metaphor. We are approaching an era when that ancient dictum to "Know Thyself" may become a reality.

What are some of the predictions that this view of the mind would make?

Intelligence is embodied.

Concepts are the basic building blocks of our thought, and the bridge between thought and language. Many basic concepts came about because of the physical nature of our species.

That study and knowledge of our concepts and how they are formed and utilized will make us more accurate and better thinkers.

That the realization that some concepts are constructs, without physical reality, will stop us from pointless disagreement about certain subjects, or guide debate, at the very least. The attempt should be made to give concepts a physical or operational basis, as in our discussion above, where *concept* can be understood as a mental representation in the brain that may be imaged and studied. Again, if concepts are the building blocks of thought, examining concepts and the ways in which they are being utilized is always a good way to begin study of almost any area of interest.

That recognition of the ubiquity of metaphor in language, and the ways it is used to expand that same into abstract realms, will allow us to find more useful and novel comparisons, and deepen our thought. This mechanism also highlights how the physical world is at the base of language. Guy Deutscher's book outlines metaphoric expansion of language in great detail. The more we know about how our language works, the more accurate our thought processes.

That there is a definite strong link between symbol usage and mode of consciousness. I would argue, and hope the reader has been convinced, that symbolic understanding is a large piece of the puzzle to our type of consciousness. This has been true historically, and it is true now. This is the age of the symbol, near the beginning of our realization of its full potential.

That there has been a trend in our symbolic worlds towards better and closer models of reality. Once there were sketches, then paintings, then photographs, then videos. Once we only told each other stories, then we wrote them, now we experience them in movie form. Deeper and more comprehensive forms of virtual reality are on the way, springing from our realization that symbols can be used to create ... anything. A time may come when the line that divides virtual and real is practically extinguished. Though, as a writer of fiction, this is not meant to demean that art and craft in the slightest. One of the wonderful things fiction allows–you might even say demands–is the use of imagination. A good writer brings you into a world, and creates a vision so real you *see* it. You *imagine* it. I don't think written fiction can or will be replaced, but that we will simply have additional options.

That artificial intelligence will almost certainly come about, and it will, of necessity, occur by teaching, using the real world as corrective device and instructor. Organisms develop and pass on various modes of thought that have survival value. This connection to the world must be established before a machine can be truly said to think. That, as has occurred in the past, and certainly is happening today, we will rely more and more on technology to enhance us, body and mind. My view is that humanity, through technology, will move closer and closer to being a symbiotic mixture of natural and artificial intelligence.

David Deutsch is a rock star in the world of physics and deservedly so. In *The Beginning of Infinity*, Deutsch states his belief that the prime determinant of the scientific method is not induction from experience, but good explanations. That all our experience is theory-laden (which I believe also, as stated in the earlier section about the senses) and that our existent theories are the determinant factor in obtaining new ones. When an existing theory doesn't explain all the phenomena in a given area, we look for one that does. I agree with this, as far as it goes, but believe it still begs the question. What changed in the human mind that moved us into the scientific realm and made good explanations even possible?

I believe that this change was the abstraction of our thought brought on by literacy, which made our concepts and words objects with permanency and stability; allowed uniformity and the ability to build complex abstractions on top of concrete, and also gave us outer artificial memory storage.

Deutsch is obviously a brilliant man and scientist, and many of his conclusions are original and thought-provoking. And his comparison of scientific exploration to the conjuring of a magic trick, in which we search behind appearances for an explanation, is the most apt extended analogy concerning science I have ever read. I do believe that scientists and physicists are, as are we all, inclined to lean toward solutions to problems within their own areas of study, and the study of language and thought, per se, *are* somewhat outside the realm of physics. It has also struck me prior that mathematicians and physicists who deal often with mathematical formulae seem inclined towards the computational view of thought, and to discount the embodied, though this is just a generalization, of course. (Great thinkers, capable of long and complex trains of thought, might place more emphasis on that process.)

Deutsch's contention that the tradition of rational critical thought brought on by the Enlightenment was responsible for the changes brought, is true, I think, as far as it goes. My contention, again, is that at the base of that movement to better explanations was the change in manner of thought and development of abstract concepts due to the rise of literacy. And, that this was actually the second time that movement occurred, the first being in Ancient Greece, and for the same reason: the rise of literacy. Though the ancient full potential was never completely realized. Perhaps this background is just taken for granted, though readers of these pages could justifiably opine that I don't believe it should be.

I must also finally say that I believe David Deutsch's discussion of morality, in which evil may always be characterized by lack of relevant knowledge of some type, seems right on the mark. A sociopath who commits terrible crimes may know all the facts, etc. that the rest of us do, but he lacks the emotional knowledge of empathy and the full knowledge of his humanity. In considering other possible examples, the lack of knowledge could always come into play in some manner. There *is* a reason that *emotion* is now often characterized as a type of *intelligence*. The same holds true with social intelligence. This theory, if correct, finally might unite *is* and *ought*, and seems reasonable to me, though I am sure some would argue it is too much so.

I do believe whole-heartedly in the unification of knowledge in all disciplines. The universe is a whole, and our "slices of the pie" always somewhat arbitrary and misleading.

I recently came across an analogy in which our body of knowledge was pictured as an island. As it grows and expands, the shoreline representing the borders of our ignorance expands as well. I do not believe this analogy is completely apt. Every day that passes we know more about ourselves and the world in which we live. As our knowledge increases, our ignorance lessens. The way the argument ran, every time we discover something new, it raises questions we could not ask before. Although there is some truth in that statement, knowledge is cumulative. We know more about the world we live in than ancient tribes did. I have every confidence that intelligent beings, hopefully including humans, will in the future know more than we do today. Each new discovery may bring fresh questions, but each new discovery increases the sum total of the knowledge we possess.

In defense of the analogy, a distinction must be made between the concepts of knowledge and truth. When I speak of knowledge I refer to scientific knowledge (or possible scientific knowledge), mainly, which is concerned with observation, the collection of data, and hypotheses about that data to form theories, make predictions. Knowledge that is concrete and usable. Useful truths. The concept of truth seems more flexible to me, and more similar to the narratives that we weave: truth concerns the agreement of a statement and the world and these statements *may* be *true* in many varied ways. Though large numbers of these may constitute knowledge, facts are not always useful distinctions. One of my favorite thinkers of all time, Robert Pirsig, made the point many years ago that the number of facts may be infinite. That the trick is in *which* facts you select.

Reality, symbols, consciousness, concepts, knowledge, intelligence: none of these is non-controversial, and volumes and volumes have been written about each, but I didn't want to get bogged down in this work with logic chopping proofs of a philosophical nature. Humans tend to learn and remember the "gist" of things, not the specific words, and I believe the gist of this piece to be largely correct, in essence, even if my language and phrasings are not, always. One of the problems a writer faces is that their inner knowledge can sometimes unconsciously and seamlessly fill in gaps on the page while the actual words don't tell the reader all they need to know. Or sometimes the things the writer knows are taken to be common knowledge but are not. These can lead to a kind of "snow blindness" of the page, where errors of omission occur. For that and any other errors, I ask indulgence. But in the end, as stated in the beginning, this is generally the way I believe the mind works. Is this piece comprehensive? It is more like a sketch of the general framework I believe exists. At my age, sometimes thoughts of mortality weigh in, and I wanted to get this framework published and *out into the world.* It has truly been a labor of love. Perhaps, if the fates (and readers) are kind, I may get the opportunity to expand on these thoughts at a later date.

Is the search for knowledge open ended and infinite? My desire is to reply "yes," because that is the way I would wish things to be, but I think it remains very much an open and interesting question. Can we know reality in some ultimate way? Is instantiation of symbolic development as artificial intelligence the ultimate step in that development? Or perhaps only the beginning of another journey that we cannot even vaguely imagine now? Only time may tell.

I have also read learned scientists who do not see how we will ever escape our particular miniscule island in the universe, due to the vast distances and technical difficulties involved. I do not believe this will remain true either. We are a species that has made a career out of escaping known boundaries and expanding frontiers.

Glossary

Abstraction

The forming of higher level generalizations by "abstracting" or emphasizing common features and ignoring differences.

Category

A category is a class of objects, events, actions, states, or mental constructs of some type.

Concept

Concepts are mental representations of categories. It is important to note, that when used in this sense, an actual physical brain state is linked to each concept, and thus this concept is not a construct, but a physical reality.

Construct

A construct is a concept that we postulate because it serves our purpose, but has no actual physical reality. Examples of constructs are concepts such as gravity, intelligence, and mind.

Induction

Framing a generalization from a finite number of observations.

Intelligence

Intelligence has been defined many ways. It is a construct. The ability to reach goals by solving problems is one good definition.

Operational Definition

An operational definition is one that can be measured or validated in some way.

Metaphor
A metaphor is a part of language not used in a literal sense

Mind
Mind is what the brain does.

Reification
Reification is the treatment of a construct (see above) as if it actually has physical existence. This can be an endless source of confusion.

Sign
Signs are events or objects that indicate another event or object by association of one kind or another. Clouds often indicate rain, and smoke often means the presence of fire.

Symbol

A symbol is an object or sign that means more than it is, in a physical sense. Points to another part of the universe besides itself.

Thinking

Thinking could be defined as the formation and combination of concepts. Even recognition of an object is an implicit combination, a statement of existence.

Truth

Truth may be defined as a statement which points out a state of affairs that really does obtain in the world. This, broadly speaking, is known as the correspondence theory of truth.

Below are the major influences on this work. I have tried also to note or mention them in the text at every appropriate spot.

Bibliography

Baars, Bernard and Gage, Nicole (2010) *Cognition, Brain, and Consciousness* 2nd Edition Academic Press

Bergen, Benjamin K. (2012), *Louder Than Words* Basic Books

Berman, Morris (1981) *The Reenchantment of The World* Cornell University Press

Carey, Susan (2009) *The Origin of Concepts* Oxford University Press

Damasio, Antonio (1999) *The Feeling of What Happens* Harcourt, Inc.

Deacon, Terrence (1998) *The Symbolic Species* W.W. Norton and Company

Dehaene, Stanislas (2014) *Consciousness and the Brain, How the Brain Codes Our Thoughts* Penguin Group

Deutsch, David (2011) *The Beginning of Infinity* Penguin Group

Deutscher, Guy (2005), *The Unfolding Of Language* Henry Holt and Company

Elliot, Clarke (2015), *The Ghost In My Brain* Viking Penguin

Flynn, James (2007) *What Is Intelligence?* Cambridge University Press

Foucault, Michel (1970) *The Order of Things* Random House

Greenfield, Susan (2015) *Mind Change* Random House

Hawking, Stephen (2010) *The Grand Design* Bantam Books

Hawkins, Jeff (2004), *On Intelligence* Henry Holt and Company

Hayakawa, S. I. (1990), *Language In Thought And Action* Harcourt, Brace & Company

Hofstadter, Douglas (1995) *Fluid Concepts and Creative Analogies* Basic Books

Hofstadter, Douglas & Sander, Emmanuel (2013) *Surfaces and Essences* Basic Books

Lakoff, George and Johnson, Mark (1980) *Metaphors We Live By* The University of Chicago Press

Levy, David (1997) *Tools Of Critical Thinking* Allyn & Bacon

Murphy, Gregory L. (2002) *The Big Book of Concepts* MIT Press

Ong, Walter J. (2002) *Orality and Literacy* Routledge

Peikoff, Leonard (1991), *Objectivism: The Philosophy of Ayn Rand* Penguin Books Ltd

Pinker, Steven (2007) *The Stuff of Thought* Penguin

Prinz, Jesse (2002) *Furnishing the Mind* MIT Press

Thagard, Paul (1992), *Conceptual Revolutions* Princeton University Press

Thagard, Paul (2005) *Mind* MIT Press

As mentioned at the beginning of this journey, writing fiction is much different (and much less difficult, for me, in some ways) than scientific exposition. I thought readers who made it this far might enjoy a sample of the differences in styles that involves. This little story also touches upon language and symbols.

Zombies

Bond was over by the corner nook, polishing off a hoagie that reeked of pastrami, romaine lettuce hiding beneath, with Roma tomatoes layered above. Bond might be scared of some things, unlike the fictional hero, but cholesterol wasn't one of them.

Leila was draped in her favorite chair: comfortable green fabric and cushions over a base that rocked, in her usual position—the half-fetal—with her bare brown legs dangling over one side, forming arcing curves that distracted Bond even as he munched the sandwich. He vaguely remembered someone saying there were no straight lines in nature, and he agreed. Her legs were the most natural things he'd ever seen. Her head was tilted downward, and a curtain of blonde hair hung over half her face, shielding her as she studied the book in her lap. He badly wanted to bother her, but restrained himself, and tossed the last bite of hoagie in his mouth and chewed contentedly.

She hated to be interrupted when deep in thought. In many ways, she was the antithesis of the dumb blonde of popular lore. She was probably the smartest woman he'd ever known.

They'd met on a ferry on the Gulf Coast. He'd gotten out of his vehicle, like most of the folks on the boat, and gone to the railing to enjoy the view of the muddy currents rushing by, and the gulls circling and cawing, with possibilities of seeing a dolphin jump, as they sometimes did in these waters. She'd been by the rail, radiant and lovely, with the blonde hair cut short then, and time itself had seemed to pause, breath held, when she looked up and met his eyes.

She was clutching a Styrofoam cup of coffee, and she cursed: a small, sharp damn. Bond asked her if he could help in some way. She shook her head, said, "No, nothing really. Just forgot to ask them to put sugar in my coffee."

Bond had eaten in a small café earlier, and had absent-mindedly stuck a sugar packet in his shirt pocket. He remembered it then, patted the pocket to verify his memory, and brought it out and extended it to her.

Her eyebrows lifted. They were fine line etchings on her face, lightly drawn. She reached out and took the packet from his hand, tore off a corner, and added it to her drink, then swirled the cup gently to mix the sugar, took a sip. "Ah," she said, "just right. I'm not worth a damn without some kind of little sugar fix. It's one of my two vices." She had a waiflike, elfin look to her, all clean lines and translucent skin, but balanced by a generous, wide mouth and piercing green eyes with yellow flecks.

He refrained from asking her what the other vice was. It seemed too easy, though inviting: like a curve ball that hung, or the perfect setups for the spike you often saw in championship women's volleyball. Instead, he took the open adjacent spot by the rail, and they stared out at the cinnamon waters, together but separate, watching the foam froth against the boat and slide by, making the occasional comment about the scenery. Till it was time for docking and he'd returned reluctantly to his truck, and watched her climb into an older, dark green Toyota, regretful already he had let her go without her name or number or something.

But the ramp had come down then and rejoined the boat to land, and a woman in a bright fluorescent orange vest with a baton light shining in one hand began waving the vehicles off, starting with the row that Bond had his truck on. All around him engines were sputtering or rumbling to life. So he fired up his truck, clattered down the ramp, and moved on.

About 10 miles later down the road, however, he'd looked over at some small burger, fish, crab joint on the Gulf side and spotted what appeared to be that same Toyota as he rolled past. Bond had eased off the coastal highway at the next intersection, hung a u and gone back, parked in the lot next to the car, feeling vaguely like a stalker, unsure if it was even the same one. There were probably a million that color.

He paused inside the brightly lit diner entrance.

The place was packed with folks: the hum of conversation everywhere, large-shouldered waitresses in bright red uniforms hurrying briskly by carrying coffee pots, with plates of food stacked on their arms. Tourists in brightly hued Hawaiian shirts and khaki walking shorts. The clank of silverware. A huge silver and blue Marlin stretched for yards high on the brick wall behind the counter. He peered around and spotted the top of her head. She was alone in a booth. Saw her luminescent green, yellow-flecked eyes peer up at him, then widen in recognition as he approached. Bond asked if she'd like some company, hands in his pockets self-consciously. She'd tilted her head slightly sideways, studying him for a scary long moment, and he'd had the oddest feeling she could see right through him, into his core. He'd straightened, without thinking about it, as she stared up at him in appraisal. A woman like her probably got bothered everywhere. She *had a paperback open on the sea-green vinyl table even then, he remembered. She rarely went anywhere without something to read. His fate hung in the balance for what seemed a long while, time ceasing its eternal respiration once more, then she nodded almost imperceptibly, things started moving again, and he slid into the booth, one of a long row that lined the diner window, where he could see the bright-colored cars whizzing by on the highway outside. She shut the novel, somewhat reluctantly, he thought and leaned back as the waitress came to take his order. She had a steaming cup of coffee next to the book, crumpled up sugar packets beside that.*

All that had been three years ago. A boat, a cup of coffee, a sugar packet. And here they were. When he looked at her, he still thought of it as some kind of miracle. Though he managed to conceal that pretty well. It didn't do to always have people know how much you cared for them. You didn't want to hang all over somebody like an affectionate dog.

"Do you think we are what we think we are?" she asked him. She had put her book down, and was rocking, studying him in that way she had, head cocked. He looked the other way, out at the pool, through the sliding glass doors and thought about the question. One thing he'd learned about Leila was she didn't suffer fools or superficial answers gladly. He focused in. Another thing was that she loved self-referential, recursive-type questions.

"No," he said.

"Explain yourself," she responded. "Go on."

"It's been the century of the unconscious," Bond said. "Almost everybody knows by now that a lot of what is happening with anybody is going on under their awareness, beneath the surface."

"That's right," she said. "Zombies."

"Zombies?"

"Creatures that don't completely know what we're doing. Not entirely alive to ourselves."

Bond chewed his lip a moment, looked over at her, thinking. That was what was undoubtedly so interesting about Leila. She veered from the beaten path a lot. Some connection was nibbling at him. Then he got it. "Or machines are like zombies," he said.

"Machines?"

"Robots or computers, I mean. Intelligent, but not alive or self-aware. Not yet, anyway." He really didn't know enough about zombies to make fine distinctions. Though they seemed to be a rage of the age.

Her rocking sped up, a sure sign he'd struck some kind of chord. Then stopped abruptly, and her legs uncurled. She came up out of the chair like a spring and got close to him, in his face. His breath quickened, the way it did every time she got close. She moved like a spring and smelled like springtime, he thought.

"Did you know we're domesticated?" she asked him, aquiline nose only inches from his. Her lips, those sweet lips, were pursed. He focused again, or tried.

Fought the urge to grab her, successfully, at least for now.

"We're a couple," he said, spreading his arms, palms up in supplication.

"Not us, clown, the race," she responded. "Civilization is just another word for domesticated. You know what's wrong with that book?" She pointed behind her.

"No," he replied, and shrugged once more, somewhat dazed by the pinball caroms of the conversation. "What's wrong with that book?"

"It's just words," she replied. "The words never get to all this." She gestured around at the house, the room, perhaps the world, he wasn't sure. He couldn't take it any longer. He grabbed her and pulled her to him.

"This isn't just words," he said, and she smiled up at him like he was a good pupil and had surprised her.

"Exactly. Exactly right," she murmured as they held each other. They were rocking slightly in place, dancing slowly without music. Then she looked up at him again and said sternly, seriously, "There's a wildness inside us, a place the words can only talk about, never get to." Her green eyes were searching his as if to make sure he understood.

He realized suddenly it was absolutely true; that he'd known that all along, though he'd never had the explicit thought before. Because at times he'd sought the wildness, the places without words. There weren't that many left, and they weren't always easy to get to. And it was the wildness inside that matched and sought them out. That which was never captured by a name.

She was watching him, still, and he had the eerie feeling again she'd read his mind. He nodded solemnly down at her, and then the words stopped for a while, as they just danced.

About the Author

Bart Hopkins Jr. has been a surfer, mountain hiker, occasional rock climber, chess enthusiast, motorcyclist, and student of language and mind and brain topics, among other things. He is the proud father of two grown children, Krystal and Bart, grandfather of three, and lives with his wife Kat in Texas.

He finds himself in the position of the Scarecrow of Oz, in some ways, with no particular academic credentials to lend credence to this work, just a boundless curiosity and nearly fifty years of private research and reading. In the way of scientists, he believes in skepticism and scientific proof. That the best method to further examine this piece is through checking it against other sources and research and coming to an informed opinion.

The *Sign* novels below deal with the major important eras of symbolic change, and are available currently. *Playtime*, *Game Time,* and *Beach Town Boogie* are novels of suspense, with the usual somewhat harsher language and bolder characters. Although the author has endeavored to make them enjoyable for thinkers as well. As a novelist and permanent student, he has found that language is a complex and variable tool, and he's used it in different manners, if poorly at times, in different contexts. And as has been said many times before, context is everything!

He believes that knowledge is good and essential, and will leave this world in current form content if he can contribute in some miniscule way to that. Even mighty mountains are made from minute grains of dirt and rock.

Also by Bart Hopkins Jr.

Fiction:

Chasing Sunlight
Sign Changes
Sign Journeys
Playtime
Game Time
Beach Town Boogie

"Life is short, art long, opportunity fleeting, experience treacherous, judgment difficult." — *Hippocrates*